I CAN'T HELP SMILING

To my friends Nell and Eileen and
Frances and Desmond McCreery

I would like to express my sincere thanks to Gloria Hunniford for writing the Foreword to this book.

My thanks also to all my friends for their encouragement and good wishes and to all the wonderful people who wrote to me expressing appreciation of my last book and their good wishes for the success of this publication.

Rosaleen Davies

I CAN'T HELP SMILING

Rosaleen Davies

Blackstaff Press

Published by Blackstaff Press Limited, 255A Upper Newtownards Road, Belfast BT4 3JF.

Printed inNorthern Ireland by Belfast Litho Printers Limited.

ISBN 0 85640 148 X

Contents

Foreword

I can't help smiling when I think of Rosaleen Davies' poems — nor can I think of a more apt title for this new collection. That's the effect she has on people — you simply can't help smiling at the way she treats everyday situations and brings them alive with her individual stamp of colour and humour.

I remember very clearly the first day Rosaleen arrived by bus from Annalong at the BBC studios. She hadn't done much broadcasting at that stage and I think she was bewildered as to why we wanted her to come to the city to recite some of her poems. She didn't think people would be all that interested — how wrong she turned out to be! She has this wonderful, open, smiling face and although she appeared happy enough on the outside, she admitted to me just before the red light went on that she had never been so terrified in her life. Yet once the introductions were made Rosaleen was off, relating one of those marvellous situations which we can all identify with, like 'The Doctor's Waiting Room' or 'Makin' the Right Choice'. But it would be wrong to assume that Rosaleen always writes to make you laugh: in fact, quite the reverse, because she has this great facility of stirring up all the emotions, be it nostalgia, happiness or sadness. To me that's the secret of a good writer of songs, prose or poetry — to get across on all levels. Perhaps it's her love and understanding of her native Co. Down and its people which gives her this all round depth of awareness of life which she transfers to words so easily.

It has been a privilege to write this short foreword — it has been an equal privilege to work with Rosaleen, to highlight her work and, most of all, I know you will enjoy 'smiling' your way through the following pages.

Gloria Hunniford

Marriage

The young ones goin' nowadays
Have marriage on the brain,
But it's not all love and kisses
And the changin' of your name.
Aye, it's not a bed of roses,
As some would have you think,
Just count the hours a woman spends
Beside the kitchen sink.

The ould boy clocks around the fire,
The childer scream and shout,
Till Ah'm almost at me tethers end
And give each one a clout.
It's 'gimmy this' and 'hand me that',
Ah'm more a robot than a wife,
Ah've got so used to givin'
It's become a way of life.

Ah'm bakin', cookin' washin'
From mornin' until night.
Ah think Ah'll join the Women's Lib.
And get some things put right.
There's no half-days or holidays,
Or words of thanks or praise.
For all the work Ah have to do,
Each week, for seven days.

Ah tell them that they're selfish,
An' they all should help me out,
But the childer want to go and play
And the ould boy walks about.
Ah didn't realise me luck,
When Ah lived in single bliss,
Now Ah'm just an unpaid sarvint,
Called Mrs, instead of Miss.

1

Ah envy all the weemin,
Who missed their Mr Right,
Troth Ah've got me eyes opened
And have truly seen the light.
Ah've threatened many hundred times,
to pack me bag and go,
But sure Ah know Ah'd miss them
And well, he's a civil crature Joe.

Sarah Jane's First Visit To The Cinema

Ah took Sarah Jane to the Pictures.
She'd never been there before,
It was a sort of a treat for her birthday,
She was just goin' on seventy four.
Ah mind the night well, 'twas a Thursday,
And a Cowboy film was on,
When Ah think back on it now
Ah know we should never have gone.
We left the house right and early,
As the film started at eight,
Sarah Jane was a trifle excited
And didn't want to be late.
She knew nothin' of Chaplin or Garbo,
And other film stars which we love,
The only stars she had heard of
Are the ones that twinkle above.
Ah was glad the film was a Western,
It would be at least kind of 'mild',
But Ah'd overlooked the guns and the horses,
And Sarah's innocence, like that of a child.

Goin' in she got lost in the darkness,
Missed her foot for she just couldn't see,
Then she was busy sayin', 'Excuse me,'
For she'd sat down on some fella's knee.
The people around us got angry,
And told us both for to shush,
Then some rough lookin' character
Yelled, 'Shut up!' and gave us a push.
At last, and mind Ah was thankful,
We found a couple of seats,
Ah'd just about got meself settled
And passed her a wee bag of sweets,
Then Ah noticed she was sittin' above me,
An' Ah whispered, 'Quick, pull your seat down.'
She couldn't understand my meanin'
So Ah knew that Ah'd have to turn round
To explain how the seat operated,
An' how much more comfy she'd be.
Then she landed down with a clatter
And all eyes were turned round towards me.
The screen suddenly caught her attention,
And she shouted, Look, there's Robbie's mare,
D'ye mind, Willie, he took it last week
To sell at the Halloween Fair.'
'That's not Robbie's beast,' Ah said kindly,
Then she said, 'Look at them hussies there,
They should be ashamed of themselves
They're as bold as brass and near bare.'
There was a noise as some of the horses
Set off at a very fast trot,
'Whoa there, now, whoa,' shouted Sarah
An' was surprised when they didn't stop.
From the saloon came a mean lookin' Cowboy
And in his right hand was a gun,
Before you could say, 'Bob's yer Uncle'
Sarah was out of her seat at a run.
She'd reached the street when Ah caught her,
Says Ah, 'What on earth's all the fuss?'
Says she, 'It was him with the gun
He was pointin' it right over at us.'

3

She'd no interest in seein' more of the film
Ah couldn't leave her out there on her own.
'Look,' Ah says, 'we'll have a fish supper
An' walk at our leisure back home.'
She said she enjoyed the supper,
An' Ah saw a wee smile on her face.
'I think I'm too old to watch films.
An' my behaviour was a downright disgrace.
You see, Willie, my screen is a big one,
It's the mountains, the sea, and the sky,
It's the ebb and flow of the tide,
An' a brook goin' hurrying by.
It's the sun peepin' o'er the horizon,
It's dewdrops like pearls on the grass,
It's the romantic light of the moon,
Which shines on each lad and his lass.
It's each little rabbit and squirrel,
A gull's cry or the song of a bird.
Where each cry and note has a meanin'
I suppose to you all this seems absurd?
But all nature is a Theatre of pictures,
Which change many times every day,
These are the films that I like,
I'm too old to be changin' my way.'

The Doctor's Waiting Room

I listened aghast
To all that passed
In the Doctor's Waitin' Room.
There was gossip and rumours,
Of weddin's and funerals
And how the pound hit a record boom.

They say new laws on divorce
Are to come into force,
That'll bring a smile instead of a tear.
There was Mrs Brown's Will
And those on the pill,
It's amazin' the things that you hear.

'He's in good form the day,'
I just heard someone say,
It's the Doctor, of course, that they mean.
Aye, he still likes a feg,
You're pullin' my leg,
A pipe! That I'd like to have seen.

Mrs Green's new arrival,
Which isn't surprisin',
It's her ninth, let's give her a cheer.
Joe says he wants ten,
Isn't that typical of men?
It's amazin' the things that you hear.

The film on Telly,
Which baffled our Nellie,
It dealt with the 'birds and the bees',
Now the stork is in doubt,
Gooseberry bushes are out,
Will someone explain it all, please.

Poor Lizzie's pains
And varicose veins,
Wee Henry's love for the beer.
Johnny's delight,
At the wife's sudden flight.
It's amazin' the things that you hear.

The widow's romance
With that artist from France
They say she's older than him.

That cough of young Hilda's
The red flu that near killed us
And inflation still looks very grim.

The ten penny Pan
Has got out of hand
It's now almost 30p.
Who's hoodwinking who?
For I haven't a clue
And it's certainly not Mrs T.

I'm next to go in
After Mrs McMinn
'Oh, don't worry, that's alright, dear
No, you can go on
I'll have a wee word with John
For it's amazin' the things that you hear.'

My Tomato Plants And Me

Someone said, 'have a go'
And perhaps you could grow
Lettuce, tomatoes and beet.
So I got plants and seed
With instructions to read
And pressed them down in moss peat.

Alas, that was in May,
Autumn's now on the way,
And not a tomato in sight.
I stuck rods here and there
And said the odd prayer,
Must be something I didn't do right.

I've talked to them sweetly
And whispered discreetly,
As one friend hinted I should,
But they just don't listen
Or else, something's missin,
So instead I'll say something rude.

I've had quite a shock
For behind a large stock
Two pitiful green things I see,
It's the tomatoes I shout,
But there's no one about
Except my tomatoes and me.

My Cathedral

I'll make this Mourne my Cathedral,
A Mountain peak its spire
The songs of larks and linnets
Will together form the Choir.
The sky will be the ceiling
With its ever changing scene,
The tide with its many lessons
Will be the Rural Dean.

The wind will be the Organ
With notes both soft and loud,
And for the Chandelier I'll have
A rainbow coloured cloud.
Green fields will be the carpet,
A fall of snow a Surplice white.
The moon and stars will light the way
Through the very darkest night.

Slieve Donard will be the Pulpit,
Slieve Bignian the Reading Desk,
Purple heather will be the Pews
Where one can kneel or rest.
The flowers will answer 'AMEN'
To the tall trees Creed and Prayers,
And all the many little hills
Will be the Belfrey stairs.

A winding lane will be the Aisle
And the sun will be the clock,
A cuckoo will ring the bell
To summon the scattered flock.
All the leaves will whisper
The Blessing with a sigh,
And nature bow in reverence
To the King who reigns on high.

The Fall Of Night

I've often watched the sun
Sink behind the hill,
And felt that awe and wonder
As though the world stood still.
A silent coloured picture
No canvas could portray,
The deepening shades of evening
Draws to a close another day.
But first the falling twilight,
The nightly debut of the stars,
Which light the highway of the night
Through our silent slumbering hours.
The moon emerges like a Queen,

A Monarch on high,
And beams down on her subjects
From her palace in the sky.

Love Is Blind

What did Maggie see in him
Was all that you could hear,
As he wouldn't spend the daylight hours
He's that miserable and near.
But that's not all, I tell you,
For the look of him's enough,
Wi' that awful hairy face and chest
And that smelly pipe he puffs.

You could go to Bellevue any day
An' for sure you couldn't swear,
If you were seein' Maggie's Willie John
Or a great big grizzly bear.
He grunts when he is spoken to,
Treats poor Maggie like a fool,
An' if she asks a favour
He's as stubborn as a mule.

They say that marriage opens
Every woman's eyes,
Why is it they're all so blind
An' then suddenly so wise.
At a very recent weddin',
Instead of sayin', 'I will',
The Bride said, 'No, you take him,
For I have had my fill.'

9

The Snowflake

I watch from my window
As the snowflakes fall,
And a haunting silence
Descends over all.
Twilight is falling
Yet the world is white,
And won't be changed
By the darkness of night.

The flakes come faster
As though in a race,
Making intricate patterns
Like hand-woven lace.
The firelight flickers,
Turns the white into gold,
And a feeling of warmth
Helps to shut out the cold.

Makin' The Right Choice

It's time you thought of marriage
Said me Ma till me one day,
You'll have to look out for a wife
Before your hair turns grey.
As for me, Ah'm gettin' on in years,
An' not fit till work the fields.
It's just as much as Ah can do
To prepare and cook the meals.
So look for a girl that's strong

An' willin' to pull her weight,
There's always Jenny McCrum
She'd do in a pinch, if you're bate.
She's not much to look at for sure,
But you're no oil paintin' yourself,
Ah don't think she'd dare turn you down,
She's afeered of bein' left on the shelf.
Her Da's a few quid in the Bank,
From the time he was out in the States,
Why don't you stroll over the night
Sure your Da and Henry were mates.
Aye, ould Henry's civil and quiet
And Jenny keeps a clean house,
She's always been used to hard work
So would make you an ideal spouse.
Of course there's Biddy McKay
The widow from near Meadow Hill,
You'd have to spruce yourself up
To get her till answer, 'Ah will.'
Ah don't like the strut of her walk,
She's a 'show off' from head till feet
If she'd a feather stuck here and there,
T'would be a peacock you'd see on the street.
Or what about Paddy's wife's cousin,
Her that's just back from New York,
They say she's salted a fortune
In a big Irish Bank down in Cork.
There's Nellie O'Neill down the road
You could always ask her for a lark,
But is there wan person who knows
If her hair's blond, red, or dark.
An' she's kinda long in the tooth
If you understand what Ah mane.
But sure the difference in years,
In the end might be your lucky gain.
It's a pity she's got such big hands
And a squint like her twin sister Kate,
And yet in spite of all this
She's as full as can be of consate.
You've got a good figure me lad

But alas, you've a wee empty heart.
Wan thing, Ah'm not stayin' here,
Ah'll tell you that for a start.
You'll have to move in and live
Wi' the woman you finally choose
But sure you'd nothin' to start wi'
So, therefore, you've nothin' to lose.
Och, aye, Ah'll miss you sometimes
But Ah'll sell the house and the farm,
An' buy a nate wee cottage
Not too far from the road at Glenarm.
Ah never had much of a life
Since the day Ah was daft and got wed,
An' all through the years it got worse
Till your Da finally took to his bed.
But now, thank goodness, that's over,
At last Ah can say that Ah'm free,
With only one little worry
An' that little worry is me.

The Constant Stream

The murmur of a little stream
Is music to the ear,
An Orchestra playing softly
With notes so crystal clear.
It brings both peace and comfort,
And whispers words of cheer,
It helps to soothe an aching heart
And wipes away a tear.
It's restful in its rhythm,
Like an old time Minuet,
But then the tempo changes,

We must forgo our tête-à-tête
It plays and sings so many songs,
Its good at Lullabys,
But if you try to hold it back
You hear its gentle sighs.
It races blindly onwards,
With its most unusual beat,
Not pausing for a moment
Until the rolling sea it meets.
And on its steadfast non-stop flow,
The reeds and rushes quiver,
But this lovely melody lingers on
To-day, next year, forever.

The Priest And The Vicar

The Priest and the Vicar
Had a little tête-à-tête,
And eventually the talk got round
To the Churches constant debt.
'What's your views,' asked the Priest,
'For gathering the money in.—
Apart from the plastic bucket,'
Said he, with an impish grin.
'A good question,' said the Vicar,
'And one I always dread.
Yes, finance is a constant problem,'
And he laughed and stroked his head.
'But I'm a great believer
In Sales of Work and Teas.
And money seems to roll in
Like a balmy summer breeze.'
'You're lucky,' said the Priest,

'I wish I had your touch,
No matter what I threaten
My crowd only give so much.
I shout and preach damnation
Safe behind the Pulpit rail,
It's not Sales of Work and Teas I need
But a ruddy great big pail.'
'Take my advice,' said the Vicar,
'And give the Teas a go.
Believe me, before you know it,
You'll be raking in the dough.

The Annual Gift

It popped up every birthday
For thirty years or more,
I used to get so angry
I threw it on the floor.
It came in various colours
Green, yellow, blue and cream,
I got so sick of seeing it
I used to stand and scream.
It was wrapped in coloured paper,
With a very dainty bow,
And a silly stick-on label
Which said 'use me and you'll glow'.
I used to dread that annual thud
And the Postman at the door,
I'm thinking that by this time
I must have almost thirty four.
It always bore a gift card,
With love from Auntie Kay.
But I could hardly wait

To give the ghastly thing away.
Some day I might be lucky,
At least, I'll live in hope,
Perhaps she'll send me something else
And not that bar of soap.

A Sense Of Peace

One is awed by the peace
And the sense of release,
The warmth of embrace
Though we can't see the face,
It's just a wonderful feeling.

It's the sea and the sky,
It's Hello and Good-Bye,
The sparkle of eyes
At a pleasant surprise,
It's really a wonderful feeling.

You think you're alone,
In the peace of your home,
But someone is there
Who really does care,
It's such a wonderful feeling.

You've got worries and care,
Try not to despair,
For God's close at hand,
Let Him take command,
This gives you a wonderful feeling.

Me And My Grocer

Good Morning Sam,
Two slices of ham,
And a loaf the smallest you've got.
A piece of fresh cheese,
What price is it, please?
Yes, it has turned out rather hot.

Some wheat meal and flour
What's that in the jar?
I might buy that for myself,
It's 70p?
Well between you and me,
You can put it back on the shelf.

A pound of butter and lard,
Aren't those scones a bit hard?
Those meat pies look kinda flat.
Last week they cost twenty
And dear knows it was plenty
Could you spare a wee bite for the cat?

Half a pound of good tea,
Are you givin' this free?
No, that wouldn't happen in here.
I'll have four tins of rice
And to pot with the price
And two tins of that lager beer.

I want a white spool
Now look here, I'm no fool,
40p, you're havin' me on?

But it's only just thread
Oh, forget what I said,
On inflation we'll never agree.

I see tinned fruit's on offer
And I'd be a bad shopper
If I didn't have some of that.
Throw in a wee chop,
Now I think that's the lot,
Did you remember the bite for the cat?

You've got a new till,
Well, tot up my bill.
£5, is that what you said?
But that cannot be,
And I simply don't see,
Well, try tottin' it up in your head.

The figure's the same?
Well, now who's to blame?
Denis Healey, or big brother Jim?
It's these government blokes
Who try to fool folks,
But my grocer, no one fools him.

Lookin' For A Wife

Ah've ploughed all day, Ah'm ready till drop
It's no aisy job puttin' in the crop.
There's a heifer sick, that'll mane a late night
An' them hens and turkeys'll be needin' a bite.
Betsy the mare has lost a shoe,
Ah'm in a quand'ry, Ah've that much till do.
Wan cow's in calf, ach, Ah'll not see me bed,
An' two wee terriers have yet to be fed.
The pigs can wait till the morra morn
But Ah'll throw the hens a lock of corn.
The bullocks are happy out on the grass,
But Ah've a thirst for a big pint glass.
Ah daren't go near the town the night
Ah'll be workin' here till near daylight.
Farmin's hard work when you're on your own,
Attendin' the stock, an' plantin' an' sowin'.
Should Ah look for a wife, or am Ah too old?
Mind you she'd hif to do as she's told.
Ah'd look right well wi' a wife on me arm,
An' troth at night Ah'd always be warm.
Aye, maybe a wife is what Ah need,
She could milk the cows an' give them their feed,
Clean the house and cook the food,
An' chop the odd wee bit of wood.
Aye, a woman would be handy to have about,
As long as she's quate an' not given to shout.
Ah'll dress meself up for the very next Fair,
An' if Ah'm lucky Ah might meet someone there.
But if Ah don't, Ah'll sell the whole lot,
Aye, ivery mortal thing that Ah've got.
Horses and cattle and all that Ah own,
For Ah'll not spend another Winter me lone.

The Festive Season

Red berried Holly,
Streamers galore,
A sprig of Mistletoe
Above the door.
Christmas Cards
With Santa and Sleigh,
The exchanging of gifts
Make a wonderful day.

Air crisp with frost
On this Christmas Morn,
The day we remember
Our Saviour was born.
A few flakes of snow
Like a thin white veil,
Go fluttering past
The window pane.

The arrival of friends
With wishes sincere,
Handshakes and smiles
And the odd little tear.
The day marches on
There's the odour of food,
Turkey and Ham
And the favourite Plum Pud.

Our silhouettes
In the candle light,
A background of Carols
With 'Silent Night'.
Yule logs in the hearth,
The flickering flames,
A toast to friends,
The party games.

A switch is pulled
The tree is aglow,
Presents are stacked
On the floor below.
A gift for all,
For the children a toy,
On this special day
Of peace and joy.

Left In The Lurch

Ah'm supposed to get hitched before Easter
At least that's the rumour goin' round
But this past week Ah've got a sickncr,
The thought of marriage can get a man down.
Ah've lived all me lone this ten years
An' Ah'm used to bein' me own boss
But wi' this dark cloud gettin' nearer
Ah'm not the same man that Ah was.
Ah'm smothered wi' future 'in laws'
Ah just know Ah'm doin' the wrong thing
An' Ah'm fed up wi' endless rehearsals
Of psalms and hymns we're to sing.
They've called in the local Soprano
To sing 'Ah sweet mystery of Life'—
Troth an' it'll be the greatest mystery ever
If Bridget McCann is iver me wife.
Ah know the Weddin' March backwards,
All the prayers includin' the Grace,
Ah'm sick listenin' to weemin arguin'
Over silk and satin and lace,
An who stands where at the Altar,
Who sits on which side of the Church,

For two pins Ah'd run off the night
An' lave the whole lot in the lurch.
There's Maids of Honour an' Page Boys
Who've been warned about the Bride's Train,
Could this all be a horrible nightmare
Or am Ah slowly goin' insane?
Her Da's in a terrible hurry
He can't wait till give Bridget away,
He's a wee bit too keen for my likin'
That's wan sure thing Ah can say.
To tell you the truth, Ah'm not happy,
Ah can feel the walls closin' in,
She an' her Ma took me for a sucker
But Ah'll change their smirk an' their grin.
Ah'm not all that fussed about weemin,
An' was kinda talked intil this match,
Ah suppose nobody else would take her
It's no wonder, she's not a great catch.
There's a boat leaves the night for Glasgow,
Ah'll be on it as sure as you're born,
If Ah'm lucky no one will miss me
Well, at least not till the morra morn.
She can get someone else for a husband,
Ah'd warn him if Ah knew who he'd be,
On the other hand, why should Ah worry
For wan thing's certain, it will not be me.

The Confessions Of
Wee Hughie

Wee Hughie had a word wi' the Vicar
As he wasn't feelin' too well
He didn't know much about Heaven
But was kinda frightened of hell.
Says he, 'It may come as a shock, Sir
But Ah'm thinkin' of changin' me ways,
Ah'm now past the seventy mark
An' nearin' the end of me days.
Ah've not always been strictly honest,
Ah was bad when Ah could have been good,
Ah've done many things that Ah shouldn't,
An' left undone the things that Ah should.
Ah was angry wi' friends and neighbours,
An' rude when Ah might have been kind,
An' completely lost me patience
If some silly fool changed his mind.
Ah was a wee bit short now and then
When the wife and me didn't agree,
But there was wan thing in me favour,
She was the only woman for me.
Ah niver could stan' inhumanity
Whether it be to man or to beast,
An' Ah was niver wan to start fightin,
Ah respected that wee word called peace.
Ah niver showed any interest
In a craythur's class or their creed,
But wan thing Ah niver could stomach
That incurable sickness called greed.
Ah wasn't the best of Attenders
Ah left Church goin' to other folk,
Life had always treated me kindly
Ah felt religion was some sort of joke.
Now Ah'm sorry for the years Ah've wasted,
They could have been spent to advance

22

All the many good works of God,
Might He give me another chance?
Ah know it's late to be askin'
For somethin' important like this,
But suddenly the journey to Heaven
Is a journey Ah don't want to miss.'
'Don't worry Hughie,' said the Vicar
'Ah'll have a wee word in His ear,
You've confessed, so all is forgiven
And He loves you, of that, never fear.'

Gale Force

A feather on the ground
There's no movement or sound,
Then a sudden breeze
Stirs the leaves on the trees.
The breeze turns to a gale,
With thunder and hail,
Then a creeping chill
And an angry shrill
As the wind starts to roar
Round windows and door.
It screams with rage
As though in a cage,
And cries for release
Like a frightened beast.
The trees groan in despair
As their roots seem to tear,
And an evil hand
Like a vice clasps the land.

It Could Happen To You

Would you look at the dog,
What's he got in his teeth,
And what on earth
Is that underneath.
Is that my new coat
On which he lies curled?
Because if it is,
He'll not be long for this world.
Watch out for the cat
She's gone berserk
Mercy me, she's got hold
Of your brother's clean shirt.
Surely that's not the hens
On the kitchen floor,
Somebody chase them out
And close the door.
Here comes that stupid old goose,
Will you let me out
Till I give her a shoosh.
Who let the donkey out on the lane,
Put her into her house, John,
Out of that heavy rain.
Your Da said he'd be home by five,
If the cows aren't milked
He'll skin us alive.
By the way, that Parrot
Will have to be sold,
What it said to the Parson
Just couldn't be told.
Between youngsters and housework
And birds and beasts,
I wonder if my troubles
Will ever cease.

Poppin' The Question

Ah find it hard till settle
On the wan that Ah should take,
Ah'm keen on Meg and Rosie
But Kate now she can bake.
The other two are little use
Among the pots and pans,
They're good at doin' their faces
An' manicurin' their hands.
They know all the latest records,
An' disc jockeys, whatever they are,
The current trend in fashion
An' each new model car.
But all that is very little use
As you will all agree
When tryin' till earn a livin'
As a farmer such as me.
The sheep don't need a 'hair do'
Or the mare a 'dry shampoo'
The pigs and goats are quite content
An' the cows just stand and moo.
Hens can't keep time till music
But cackle all day long,
At times the ould black rooster
Croons a few bars of a song.
Aye, Kate's more till my likin'
She calls a spade, a spade,
Her head's not full of nonsense
An' she's waitin' ready made.
Aye, waitin' for the askin'
An' Ah think Ah might do worse,
If half of what folks say is true
She's got a few pounds in her purse.
An sowl a bit of money's useful
An' Ah've got the farm an' stock
An' a wheen of fivers tucked away,
In me Da's ould woolly sock.
The night Ah'll pop the question

An' hope that she'll say 'yis'
If she does we'll seal the bargain,
Wi' a great big hug and kiss.

'A Taste Of Hunni'

If you feel a bit low,
Or a bit short of dough,
Or perhaps on the verge of despair,
Switch on at 10.5
And come really alive
When Gloria's on the air.

If you've found something old,
Perhaps a small piece of gold,
Or even something more rare.
If you're anxious to know
Why your carrots won't grow
Ring, when Gloria's on the air.

She'll test your I.Q.
By asking who's who,
And who did what, when and where.
If you haven't a clue
You'll not get a sou
When Gloria's on the air.

If you're in any doubt
About rainfall or drought,
Or you want a transplant of hair,
Ring 45262,
You'll be told what to do
When Gloria's on the air.

There's Eilish and Diane,
And that nice young man
Who for discs and tapes has a flair.
They keep things going smooth
And everyone on the move,
When Gloria's on the air.

To many thousands of us
This programme's a must,
To miss it we just wouldn't dare.
There's variety galore,
And it's never a bore
When Gloria's on the air.

The Producer is pleased
With what she's achieved,
They're really a wonderful pair.
The programme's in its third year,
So let's give them a cheer,
And long may they be on the air.

Takin' A Dip

What's this I see goin' down the lane
It surely can't be Mary Jane,
That's off to sunbathe and to swim,
Och, maybe it's her brother Jim.
No, steady, that's a woman's figure,
I thought Mary Jane was bigger.
She's looking East, she's looking West
Wondering where she could undress.
She's looking North, she's looking South
She can't see anyone about.

She's heading straight for the open sea,
But goodness me this cannot be,
No clothes at all, but just a hat,
It's maybe some young silly brat.
No, that apparition's not sixteen
Yet not ashamed of being seen.
Bedad, it's Mary Jane all right,
She isn't half a funny sight.
She must feel sure she's all alone,
Standing nude against the foam,
But why the birthday suit and hat
I simply can't get over that.
While in the water she's O.K.,
But look what's headin' round the Bay,
She didn't bank on this I bet,
Three men, a boat, and fishing net.
Now in the sea she'll have to stay
Till they decide to sail away.
The motto of this little Ode,
Is bear in mind the Seaside Code,
Wear your trunks, or swimming suit,
And then you needn't give a hoot.

The Days Ahead

Out of the ashes
Will come love and peace,
Broken bodies will be made whole,
Pain and heartache will cease.
We will embrace,
We will shake hands,
We will question why,
Man made such great demands.

We have achieved nothing
But have caused anguish and pain.
Are we satisfied?
Or will we do it yet again?
We have been given a life
But let's never take one,
Show the face of a friend
Not the point of a gun.

After The Honeymoon

Ah looked across the table
An' thought, what have Ah wed?
She's like a freak from outer space
Wi' that tin plate on her head.
'Pardon me,' says she, 'them's curlers,
For makin' instant waves.'
Ah never cease to be amazed
At the fads that weemin craves.
Wan week her eyes are coloured green
The next they might be blue
It's just the same as wi' her hair
It changes colour too.
Her face at times Ah cannot see,
It's covered wi' a mask,
And if Ah try till question her,
Ah'm told Ah shouldn't ask.
She'll sit and hum, and trim and cut
Her nails for hours on end,
And try out endless lipsticks
To get the perfect blend.
You cannot see the Dresser
Wi' it's endless rows of jars,

An' umpteen perfume bottles
Wi' the names of various flowers.
Some evenin's when Ah come home tired,
Ah cannot help but wonder
If the apparition there is mine
Or have Ah made some awful blunder.
She's far from bein' a beauty
Wi' her powder and her paint,
Why must weemin try to be
Somethin' which they aint.
Wan thing is for certain,
She isn't any dream,
Wi' all her tubes and jars
Of that stuff they call cream.

The Monday Morning Blues

I look at it with longing,
Not wanting to part,
That's how I feel on Monday
When a new week has to start.
It's just the same on Tuesday,
That longing's still there,
It lasts right through to Wednesday,
I try not to despair.
It gets easier on Thursday,
When you work a five day week,
And when it comes to Friday
There's an extra special treat.
With Saturday and Sunday
There'll be a nice long lie,
Oh, happy, happy week-end
Don't ever say Good-Bye.

But, alas, a clock stands near me
With a horrible alarm,
I could easily smash the dratted thing
By stretching out my arm,
I feel sometimes I cannot face
Those Monday morning blues,
Oh, how I'd love to snuggle down
And have another little snooze.

The Grouser

Ah must take Robert John to the Doctor
He says he's a pain in his side
An' the grumblin' of men is somethin'
Ah can neither thole nor abide.
He stayed off his work for a fortnight
An' spent every day lyin' in bed,
He wasn't too ill to watch Telly
Or shout when he wanted fed.
Ah was broke buyin' fegs and tobacco
An' actin' the part of a Nurse,
An' him tryin' to make me believe
Everyday he was feelin' much worse.
Ah mind when he hurt his big toe
He'd a bandage right up to his knee,
It was sympathy that he was after,
Troth he didn't get it from me.
The time that he had the toothache
The whole house was up half the night,
But the next day at the Dentist's
He put up a very good fight,
So much so that the Dentist
For days had a very sore face.

But Robert John's tooth, let me say
Is still in the very same place.
Ah tell you, Ah'll stan' it no longer
Ah'm sick of bein' told, well, we'll see,
He can make up his mind before evenin'
For it's either the Doctor or me.

Dislikes

People full of affectation
And vanity and pride,
Trying to solve a problem
Without the proper guide.
Algebra and Geometry
Or Maths of any kind,
Seeking for that something
You know you cannot find.

Speeches long and boring,
Stretching over half an hour,
Sitting watching T.V.
When 'pop' off goes the power.
Wind that reaches gale force
And smacks the window pane,
Those who want the front seat
It's their one and only aim.

Those who think they know it all
Yet have so much to learn,
Those who love to boast and brag
About how much they earn.
Those who try to set the pace
And want the leading Role,

Those who'll stop at nothing
To gain their selfish goal.

Nell

Have you met my friend Nell?
No? perhaps it's as well
You'd never find her at home.
She's a real globe trotter,
You simply can't stop her,
She's either just comin' or goin'.

She's seen every clime,
From Hong Kong to Millisle,
She could write a brochure or two.
She's been to Uganda,
Capetown and Ruanda,
And sat in the Gardens at Kew.

She's sailed in the Queens,
Met Debs and Deans,
Including some snob VIPs,
Took Broadway by storm
And sailed round the Horn,
As well as all seven seas.

She's seen Naples Bay
At the end of the day,
'Neath the twinkling lights of stars,
The Colosseum at Rome,
And the Catacombs,
Also booked on the first flight to Mars.

She taught the Chinese
To say 'thank you' and 'please',
Among other things you can bet,
Went twice to Alaska
Because a friend asked her,
And for all I know, she's there yet.

It was always her goal
To cross the North Pole,
Aboard a large Jumbo Jet.
She wined and dined in Paree,
Learned to say 'Oh, oui, oui!'
And tried her hand at Roulette.

She's seen many places
And many strange faces,
Some thousands of miles apart,
In Annalong she'll find peace,
When her wanderings cease,
For Mourne stole a bit of her heart.

My Photograph

(*A tribute to Mother*)

The photo on the bookcase
Stands serene and calm,
The lovely memories it holds
Act like a healing balm.
The face is kind and wears a smile,
I never see a frown,
But in my lovely photograph
There's no laugh or hint of sound.

Although my photo cannot speak,
It seems to understand,
As I derive such comfort
When things get out of hand.
The eyes appear to follow me
To each corner of the room,
They anticipate my going out
And a look says, 'Come back soon.'

There's company in a photograph
When it's someone you've held dear,
But it would be cruel and unkind
To wish that it could hear.
Yet I talk to my lovely photograph
Of events throughout the day,
And each night at my fireside
It's remembered when I pray.

It's a very happy photograph
So I must not shed these tears,
Because I know we'll meet again
In the not too distant years.
There'll be so much to talk about
And things to do and see,
Yes, one person will be mother,
And the other will be me.

The Pains Of Hunger

Not a drop of milk
Or a crust of bread,
I needn't call them in
It breaks my heart
To look at them,
Their wee bodies are so thin.

Aye, times are hard
And money's scarce,
Bein' poor is hard to bear.
But it hurts you most
With the childer's cry
In your ears as they climb the stair.

I've had to beg,
For the childer's sake,
But there's them are loth to give.
They don't know the pain
Of hungry eyes
That daily ask to live.

There's not been a day
This past six months
Their wee stomachs were filled.
And there's not been
The sound of laughter
Since their father was killed.

I've just been told
I've got a job,
In the big house on the hill
Washin' and scrubbin',
It will suit me fine
And will pay the grocer's bill.

Ten shillings a week
For six days work,
It'll keep the wolf from the door,
And when the childer get bigger
They'll help to earn some more.

Just pray that you
May never know
The ache of hunger's pain,
Or the cryin' of a mother
Who has begged for food in vain.

Keeping Up With The Jones's

A country cottage is a must,
Apart from our home in town.
Would someone call at Cleaver's
To collect that slinky evening gown.
We must get a dish-washer
And that old fridge must go.
Everyone is buying freezers
So we must make a show.

We must keep up with the Jones's.

A large screen colour TV,
The latest model Rolls,
And, yes, you won't believe it
Not one, but two mink stoles.
A second car is ordered,
One simply will not do.

I hear the very latest craze
Is, not one husband, but two.

We must keep up with the Jones's.

A lorry load of antiques
Has landed at the door,
They say each house should have them
Though I find them all a bore.
A six month cruise around the world
Is arranged for the month of May,
It's hoped the neighbours will be watching
When our trunks are sent away.

We must keep up with the Jones's.

An unusual guest arrived last night
In the shape of an Afghan hound,
His job to guard the premises
By doing a nightly round.
A swimming pool in the garden
Is our very latest buy,
I can't think why we need it
And I keep on asking why?

But I'm told, we must keep up with the Jones's.

Our country home like that in town
Will have all 'mods and cons',
And with at least two gardeners
To cut the hedges and the lawns.
A private beach with golden sand
And signs with 'No Admission',
A lady's maid of au pair
Would be an excellent addition.

We must keep up with the Jones's

Let's stop this silly nonsense
And forget these things we've bought,

True happiness comes from within
It's not something we buy in a shop.
It's a chat with friends and neighbours
It's freedom from worry and care,
It's saying, thank you God, each night
In the form of a little prayer.

There's no need to keep up with the Jones's.

A Question Of Marriage

Ah'm sick and tired of questions
As to why Ah never wed,
But is it any wonder,
After all Ah've seen and read.
Ah know of them that's happy
And Ah know of them that's not,
Maybe that's why Ah was feared
Of ever bein' caught.

Ah'm not sayin' that weemin's angels,
Or that any man's a saint,
There's lots for sure on both sides
Who should be what they aint.
There's some'll tell you love is blind,
Aye, and a lot more else forby,
It's the raisin Ah'm not rushin'
For it's a hard knot to untie.

Men'll always try to tell you
A wife has nowt to do,
But their busiest day is Tuesday,
When they sign on at the Buroo.

And then they wander home again
And flop down in a chair,
It would drive a body round the bend
It's more than Ah can bear.

There's shirts and singlets to be washed
And inside drawers to steep,
The clatter on a nice clean flure
Of great big dirty feet.
There's shouts that go unanswered
When it's time to sit and ate,
How quickly men can disappear
When their grub is on the plate.

They think they're better drivers
Than any woman yet,
But that's a little something
On which Ah wouldn't care to bet.
If swearin', revvin', speedin'
Is drivin' at its best,
Then half the male drivers
Should be under house arrest.

Did you ever watch their faces
When the wife for money begs,
They should count what they spend
On drinks, and treats and fegs.
The promise at the Altar
Is for better or for worse,
But Ah'll make one suggestion
Do a little thinkin' first.

The Silent Parting

Must I leave those I love
To face the unknown,
Like a leaf in the wind
Must I go alone.
Leave these dear shores
Where each stone is a gem,
How can I live
If I don't see them?
These hills of Ahakista
And Dunmanus Bay,
The soft winds and streams
All want me to stay,
But I can't live on beauty
And work there is none,
It's only the rich
Can bask in the sun.
I've crept from my home,
I've not told a soul,
So no one knows
My ultimate goal.
I said no Good-byes,
I wanted no tears
As I couldn't depart
With those sounds in my ears.
My mother's voice
Would have uttered reproof,
But we can't all live
Under this tiny roof.
With empty stomachs
And hungry eyes,
Our poverty is honest
It can't be disguised.
One mouth less to feed
That's why I'm going,
Leaving this land
Without anyone knowing.

Is this my fate?
Is this God's will,
That I must swallow
This bitter pill?
To cross the Atlantic
To look for work,
Just a slip of a girl
Called Kathleen Burke.
Yes, I'm eighteen years,
It's time I was gone,
But I'll carry the lilt
Of an Irish song.

How Mean Can You Get

There's never been one like her
In all of County Down,
She's the meanest kind of creature
You could ever have around.
She wouldn't make a drop of tay
If you were dying on your feet,
She's anything but popular,
Wi' the people in our street.

The ould boy's feared to ask her
For a bun or piece of cake,
The look of him would scare you
You couldn't tell him from a rake.
The lives of their wee dog and cat
Are hangin' by a thread,
If it wasn't for the neighbours,
The poor things would be dead.

She goes to Church on Sunday
But she's no more generous there,
As the collection plate goes past
She just says she's none to spare.
Ah often wonder what she'll do
Wi' all that she's put by,
She cannot take it wi' her,
Though she'll have a damned good try.

The Butcher and the Baker
Lay 'odds on' every hour,
That she'll have to buy a bit of meat,
Or a bag or two of flour.
She hasn't bought a bag of coal
Or a bag of slack this year.
Her main and only worry·
Things are gettin' shockin' dear.

You dare not mention Christmas,
Such a word wi' her's taboo,
She wouldn't have a notion
Of the things that she could do.
Her world revolves around herself,
For others not a thought,
She's to be pitied wi' her money,
For that's really all she's got.

You could count the times on one hand
That she's ever paid a fare,
She'd go from here to Cork and back
By usin' Shanks's mare.
She's always cryin' poverty,
And hasn't learned the way to live,
Yet it's all so very easy
Just by knowing how to give.

The School Patrol Man

He'll give you a smile,
He'll give you a wave,
He'll make sure that drivers
And children behave.
He can stop cars and trucks,
And the odd bus and van
Yes, I'm talking about
The School Patrol Man.
He's out in all weathers,
Rain, hail or shine,
To guide children safely
Across roads in time.
You just couldn't miss him,
With his board and his hat
And in between crossings
He enjoys a wee chat.
He keeps all the kids
In his care on the hop,
With the big sign he holds
Which simply says STOP.

The River

Chuckling, laughing, chatting, whispering
Merrily as it flows along,
Lapping quietly, moving swiftly,
Often bursting into song.
Time and tides of no importance
And it follows no command,

It's a river running freely
Through this very lovely land.

Along its banks all nature blossoms,
Primrose, violets, celandine.
The furry touch of pussy willows,
Clumps of broom just in its prime.
Yet above all this wild beauty,
Soft yet clear the river speaks,
As it rushes forward, onward,
Over crevasses and creeks.

What's the rush, Oh, what's the hurry,
What is it you have to say?
Tarry with us for a moment
Let this be our happy day.
Oh, how restful is your singing,
Oh, how cool is your embrace,
As we watch our own reflection
Mirrored in your soothing face.

The Keep Fit Class

Get down on the floor,
Now lie perfectly straight,
Take a deep breath,
Breathe out, and wait.
You must learn to relax
And let yourselves go,
My goodness Dorothy,
Not that, no, no, no.
Raise one leg at a time,
No, just one, you fool
Rhythm girls, rhythm,

And keep it cool.
That's the idea, first the right,
Let it fall gently
Betty, you gave me a fright.
I meant gently and quietly
Not with a bump,
Straighten your shoulders
And get rid of that hump.
Now raise the left, up it goes
Let it down, easy does it.
Now all touch your toes.
And again, and again,
And again, and again.
Remain on your feet,
When the whistle blows
There's lots to get through
Before anyone goes.
Swing your body
From side to side
Try and watch me
I'll be your guide.
Keep time to the music
Jane, you're way off beat
Move your body,
Never mind your feet
Let's try the arms
Quickly, up and down.
Sheila dear,
Don't act the clown.
You've all come here
To try to get fit,
Not to sit in circles
And chatter and knit.
So let's start again
At the count of three,
Keep one ear on the music
And one eye on me.

A Time For Giving

Let bells ring out, let voices raise
To show our hearts are full of praise,
Rejoice with Him who reigns above
Within those realms of joy and love.

On this His birthday every year
Our message is to bring good cheer,
To spread that cheer to those in need
As this would please Our Lord indeed.

We all have something we can share
A generous heart is never bare.
Remember those whose grief is new,
There must be something we can do.

There's more to life than food and fare,
Try throwing a kind word here and there.
Give of your time, make no excuse,
Time can be put to such good use.

It's nearing resolution time,
Let's know just where to draw the line.
Don't overact, or underrate,
The strength of love, the power of hate.

Spring Cleaning

Dusters at the ready
All set for the grime,
Mops clean and tidy
It's spring cleaning time.
Have we all the requirements
To cope with the dirt,
All the cleansing liquids,
Which need only a squirt?
Mr Bright will shine
Most things you've got,
In fact, the Ad says,
He'll shine the whole lot.
For the carpets you'll need
Six hundred and one,
With all these inventions
Spring cleaning is fun!
The silly old cob-webs
Keep brushing your cheek,
It's like playing a game
Of hide and seek.
One minute you see them,
The next they're not there,
But when the sun shines
They're everywhere.
I've watched the Telly,
Bought all the new cream,
But you need elbow grease
To get things really clean.
I'm just done out
With a pain in my back,
So I'll call it a day
And hit the sack.
There's lots more to do,
And tomorrow I'll scrub,
Why must April bring
This annual hub-bub.

The Diet

I've gone on a diet
But suggest you don't try it,
As I'm down to just half my size.
I gave up eating bread
And ate wafers instead,
No one knows me in my new disguise.

I ate toast one morning
But with a grave warning,
No more for the rest of the day.
Buns and cakes are taboo,
Also plates of hot stew,
One must keep the calories at bay.

I enjoyed hunks of cheese,
But was told cut down, please,
Try a boiled egg, if you like,
No potatoes or fries
Or any meat pies
But you can have the odd little bite.

No whisky or beer
Was made perfectly clear,
A small glass of milk should suffice.
No chocolates or sweets
Or trifles or treats
Simply nothing which tastes really nice.

No Christmas plum pud
Or any choice food
Yes, a small bit of chicken or ham.
Try not to give in
And you, too, can get slim
What, not even a spoonful of jam?

I'm as weak as can be
That's if I'm really me,
At the moment I'm not very sure.
What I'd like right now
Is a big plate of chow,
Dieting I just can't endure.

There's a grave indication
I could die of starvation
But I'd rather die happy instead.
So I'll eat what I like
But get out the ould bike
And go back to good wholesome bread.

Imagination

I asked how he was,
He said he was sick,
That man's a mystery
He knows every trick.
Aye, every trick you could name
To keep him from working,
It's a downright shame.
If he's not on the sick
He's on the Buroo.
If he could fake the pension
He'd be on that too.
He complains of his head,
He complains of his back,
There's times I'd like
To hit him a crack.
He can't walk to the pub,
For he's pains in his legs,

And the sick money he gets
Wouldn't keep him in fegs.
Stoopin' and bendin'
Are things of the past
And he can't remember
When he watched football last.
There's pains in his chest,
And pains in his knees,
If he goes to the door
He starts to sneeze.
He's not all that steady
When he's on his feet,
But sure it's no wonder,
For he cannot eat.
That's what he says,
But it's far from true,
He could eat twice as much
As me and you.
The man's a fraud
He's both healthy and fit,
But I've got a sickness
And it's called the pip.

The Lonely Road

It's lonely in the winter
Tramping through the snow,
No cosy bed, or shelter,
When the icy north winds blow.
Only the darkening sky above
And the ground beneath his feet,
An aged, homeless gipsy
Shivering on his beat.

Lingering at the windows,
Where he sees a flickering flame,
Wondering why it's been his fate
To play this nightly game.
Creeping round the dust bins,
For a crust, or bite to eat,
Why is it that some folks
Have food and clothes and heat.
But then he thinks, I'm lucky
I have all the heavens above,
And all of mother nature
To surround me with her love.

The Soprano

Kitty loved to sing out at Concerts
Fancied herself, you know what Ah mane,
Ah wouldn't have called her a singer,
Ah'd have called her another name.

She tries to reach all the high notes,
But falters and sings out of tune,
Yet carries on, quite undaunted,
It gets worse when she starts to croon.

Ah close me ears, Ah can't listen
An' people start stampin' their feet,
Last week a man threw a tomato
An' that knocked her right off her beat.

When singin' she sounds like a siren,
One night six men left the Hall,
They were part time Firemen, you see,
An' thought they were racing to answer a call.

A few weeks ago at a dinner
A farmer, whose cow had been sick,
Rushed out when she just missed F sharp,
Ah never saw anyone rush out so quick.

At the Institute's Annual Supper
She was up on the platform once more.
This time it was Mrs Magee
Who made a wild rush to the door.

You see, she'd left her young baby
Wi' a friend who lives down the street,
Hearin' Kitty's 'Ave Maria'
She swore the baby had swallowed its teat.

She was asked to sing in the choir,
It was pathetic to watch Vicar's face.
The only way he could stop her
Was to finish the service in haste.

The organist was doin' a war dance,
Feet and hands flew over the keys,
But she managed to drown Kitty's singin'
An' we all flopped to give thanks on our knees.

The Goggle Box

What are your viewing habits
What programmes do you like?
There's always 'The Good Life'
Or Hattie Jacques and Eric Sykes,
The Liver Birds and Cilla,
Or 'Are you being Served',
Sometimes we get more
Than we honestly deserve.
There's lots of crime and passion,
And detectives by the score,
Colombo, Kojak, Cannon,
It could get to be a bore.
Starsky and Hutch with Huggy Bear
Rate high with all us dames,
And two favourites, Bruce and Anthea
In the Generation Games.
The immaculate Mr 'You know Who'
In that very 'Open Sale',
'This is your Life' with Eamonn,
Which never seems to fail.
'Top of the Pops', 'New Faces',
'Give me the Moonlight', Frankie Vaughan,
And all the well known singers,
Including Elton John
Let's not forget the animals,
'Bugs Bunny' and 'Lamb Chop',
And what about 'Tom and Jerry'
Who keep each other on the hop.
There was the famous 'Forsyte Saga',
And the life 'Upstairs and Down',
Or you may prefer a Western
And see them shootin' up the town.
You could switch to 'Panorama',
'World in Action', or 'Tonight',
A boring political broadcast,
On behalf of the Left or Right.

There's boxing, there's wrestling,
And 'Match of the Day',
A tête-à-tête with Michael Parkinson,
The show which often ends the day.
TV is now a way of life,
It keeps us up to date,
But spare us all I beg you,
From debates of bigotry and hate.

Rags And Riches

There was Master Fred from the Manor
An' wee Billy from down near our street,
Their ways of life were so different
One thought they were destined never to meet.
They never met in their young days
Their backgrounds were so far apart,
They weren't in the same social circle
That was a barrier right from the start.
Young Freddie was full of importance
And spoiled by his parents for sure,
He got everything that he asked for
He didn't know what it was to be poor.
He had toys of every description
And when older his own racing car,
He stepped into his father's business
Where he first held the reins of power.
Money simply slipped through his fingers
On lavish holidays abroad,
He lost thousands in Paris and Vegas
He seemed to think he was some kind of God.
He was a snob and a real nasty fellow,
His friends numbered only a few,

If you'd the time to sit down and read it
You'd find him no doubt in *Who's Who*.
Now wee Billy was a lovable person
For about as long as I mind,
He was good to his sisters and parents
And always thoughtful and kind.
He grew up without toys or presents,
He worked hard at his lessons in school,
He'd his own kind of 'code of honour',
And in everything he kept to the rule.
I think he was just about sixteen
When he heard the call of the sea,
He was lucky, he got a job on a liner
On its runs from New York to Dundee.
It was on one of these runs he met Freddie,
He'd seen him in Church when on leave,
Freddie pretended he didn't know him
But Billy found this hard to believe.
So he gave a shrug of his shoulders
And thought, it will sort itself out,
And it had in a very few minutes
By the sound of a sudden shout.
Man overboard: was all he could hear
As passengers flocked to the side.
The Atlantic is wide and it's deep
And holds terrors we couldn't describe.
Billy heard someone say it was Freddie
And without thinking he dived into the sea,
In those few seconds he suddenly thought,
'What if it hadn't been Freddie, but me.'
The barriers were all forgotten
As poor Freddie tightened his grip,
Billy put his arms under and round him
And guided him back to the ship.
Out of this sprang a wonderful friendship,
And in between trips they would meet,
There were evenings spent at the Manor,
And at Billy's home in the street.

Marry In Haste

You couldn't say that he deserved her
But he got her that's for sure.
And he never knew what pleasure was
From the day she crossed the flure.
He was feared to speak, or even smile,
Although the house was his.
For Maggie had a shockin' tongue
When her temper was riz.

Poor ould Jack was easily led,
He didn't know her type.
His friends all tried to tell him
'She's like one would "fly her kite".'
But the dattie wouldn't listen
You can't talk till them in love,
For all that they can ever see
Is the moon and stars above.

He led her to the Altar,
It was his only leading role.
She was goin' to change all that
Once she got control.
She knew he owned two farms of land
And a lot of stock to boot,
That was all she cared about,
For him, she didn't give a hoot.

She had him up each mornin'
Around the crack of dawn,
While she lay up in bed and slept
Till half the day was gone.
She wasn't one for farm work,
Bein' born and city bred.
Now he asked a constant question,
Why on earth he ever wed?

He daren't ask a neighbour
In for a chat and drop of tay,
She was never there to make a meal,
He made his own food everyday.
She got very keen on dancing
And she started playing golf.
Some pip squeak called for her each day
He heard her call him Rolf.

Perhaps someday she'll pack her bag
And return from where she came,
It would be a lucky day for Jack
For that hussy has no shame.
He's had his fill of weemin,
He only wants to live his lone.
After Maggie, who could blame him?
He couldn't call his soul his own.

The New Teacher

We got a new School Teacher,
The terror of the place,
The words, 'I'll lick you into shape,'
Were written on her face.
Her hair was tied up in a bun
She wore a long black skirt,
She was like a Major on parade,
But had a soft spot for our Bert.
She was very good at English
And a wizard at sums,
But once a week for certain
She had a visit from the Mums.
They complained about their children,

Willie John, and James and Dick,
And Sammy couldn't go to school
For half the time he's sick.
If you didn't do your homework
She made you write a hundred lines,
And if you dared to come in late
You wrote it another hundred times.
You never dared to answer back,
In school her word was law,
She wasn't scared of anything,
So no good running to your Paw.
She was very conscientious
And tried to teach us right,
And always very willing
To coach some who weren't too bright.
She was often very tired
When the lessons were through,
Yet she somehow always found the time
To tell you how and what to do.
She turned out lots of pupils
Marines and soldiers by the score,
Some were decorated
In 1944.
Some went in for teaching,
Some for nursing, some a trade,
A few just lacked the spirit
And didn't make the grade.
It isn't until later years
One learns to realise,
How very hard a teacher works
To mould and shape our lives.

Bad Tidings

She had a most peculiar grin
For everyone she met,
And once she started talkin',
She never seemed to quet.
She knew everybody's business,
What she didn't know she guessed,
She revelled in the bad news,
.And had no interest in the rest.
If you bade her a Good Morning,
She'd ask you, why 'twas good,
And if you tried to tell her,
She'd mumble something rude.
If you maybe praised a neighbour
Or said someone had done well,
She'd quickly contradict you
And send you and them to —.
It's very true and very sad
That such people do exist,
Do not condemn, but pity them
For all the love they've missed.

Radio Ulster

Perhaps you're not a TV viewer
But Radio is your line,
And to get the best of programmes
Well, you've got to watch the time.
In Ulster they're early birds
And say 'Good Morning' to us all,

The handsome Sean Rafferty
Often takes this early call.
There's a happy band of people
Who do a worthwhile job,
By keeping us right up to date
With news items from abroad.
Mike McKimm our own Reporter
Brings tit-bits from near and far,
And Helen Madden goes 'Up Country'
In her nifty little car.
Mary Clarke gets down to business
And tries to help us out,
'Consumer Desk' has many problems
That's what it's really all about.
If your roses need some pruning
And you're doubtful what to do
John Mercer is the expert
On these and other flowers too.
'Up Wards, Down Wards' was devised
To cheer the people who are sick,
Then there's Tony Martin
He'll play any record that you pick.
'What's West' from Londonderry
Is a weekly half-hour chat,
With various local people
Discussing this and that.
For my very favourite programme
No, I won't give you any clue,
Yes, of course, it's 'Taste of Hunni'
Why? well, there's Gloria,
And I've been on the programme too.

Relations

They've taken wee Ned to the hospital
He got sick and couldn't stay on his own,
But I hated the sight of yon ambulance
I was real sorry to see him goin'
He'd lived on his own since the wife died
Although he'd daughters who lived very near,
He looked back as he lay on the stretcher
And used his hand to wipe off a tear.
He knew the daughters didn't want him
And he'd never again see his wee home,
It's a hard and cruel world
When you're old, and sick on your own.
It's worse when you've sons and daughters
Who won't give up their pleasure and fun,
To nurse a sick mother or father
But, time will pass and their turn will come.
Ned was a very good husband and father
And laboured hard all his life,
He'd a cosy house down our street
And was good to his children and wife.
If a neighbour was ever in trouble,
He was first to appear on the scene
To see what help he could offer
I'll not forget what he did for our Jean.
He'd come to his gate every evening
Before locking up for the night,
Have a word with the casual late stroller
And enjoy a few puffs of his pipe.
He never asked much from this world
But he loved his work and his home,
I don't think he had any enemies
And his old rocking chair was his throne.
People couldn't understand his daughters
They were always too busy to pay him a call,
They could have shown him a little kindness
Who knows, it mightn't be for too long.

I thought they'd have made their way round
If only to say Cheerio,
But they'll soon be fighting between them
For his few wee belongings and dough.
The deep seated greed of relations
Sickens me right to the core,
Material things are so unimportant
Yet most keep on shouting for more.
Perhaps some folk could never be happy,
So need money to play with and spend,
But with all the things it can buy
I'll settle for a good solid friend.

Maggie

We stood silently in the Churchyard
As the service came to an end,
Many people around were weeping
For they knew that they'd lost a friend.
Maggie died as she lived very quietly
And was known to both young and old,
Her door was always open
And her heart was a heart of gold.
She listened to everyone's troubles
But never a secret was told,
She loved a wee chat with her neighbours
And had many a yarn to unfold.
She hadn't much when it came to money
Yet her cupboard was never bare,
If you asked her, what made her happy
She'd answer, having something to share.
If someone got sick in the nightime
It was 'send for Maggie' she'll know what to do

And with all the maternity cases
She knew exactly when each child was due.
It was the same with most of the farmers
Many a night she spent in a byre,
Helpin' out when a cow was in calf
She was one woman you had to admire,
And was one of those very rare people
Who did things without any fuss,
Pomp and pride she just hadn't time for
And would openly show her disgust.
There was one winter day at the Market,
A woman who looked feeble and old,
Stood shivering in light tattered clothing,
Even Maggie was feelin' the cold
But she took off the coat she was wearin',
And put it round the old woman's frame,
'It's all right,' Maggie said, 'I don't need it;
It will keep out the wind and the rain.'
The face that looked up to thank her
Told a story all on its own,
It bore the marks of sorrow and hunger
'Come,' said Maggie, 'and I'll take you home.'
You could fill not a book but a volume
Of Maggie's many good deeds,
She was Father Confessor, Doctor and Nursemaid
And a stranger to hatred and greed.
I'm glad that she's still remembered
For she's gone this nine or ten years,
Even yet when her name is mentioned
There are eyes which fill up with tears.
What memories will we leave behind us
What will rank as one's finest hour,
Or will we simply lie forgotten
Like the bloom from a withered flower.